Contents

Dedication

This book is dedicated to my cat, Mr. Bu. Bu was with me every single step along the way through downsizing, packing, moving, shuffling things around, getting used to the sounds and smells in the new place. And he was always talking and loving. What a cold journey this would have been without him.

If you knew as you begin a journey that you'll have enough of everything you need to be safe and secure along the way,
how would you feel about beginning your next journey?

–SARA B. HART

Prologue

The second part of the title to this book "Getting to Enough" may be confusing. What does that mean? About 20 years ago I began a project called *The Sign of Enough™*, which was designed to encourage us to work with the question "How will I know when I have enough?" At that time I was concerned about what I thought to be our culture's penchant for encouraging overconsumption to the detriment of our planet and often our own peace of mind and time spent with those things that really are important, like family, friends, our spiritual life, play. As the years have passed, I have become increasingly concerned about our ever expanding needs to acquire things and toys and big homes and cars. I'm now very worried about the huge and growing economic inequality in our country and, actually, in the world. So, having been focused on this topic for many years, I realized when I began downsizing that I had the "forced opportunity" to see what, for me, enough really looked like. And I've found that it looks much different from where I started months ago, and yet, I have absolutely everything I need, including enough space, even though my apartment is less than a quarter the size of the house I moved from. So, I invite you to think about your opportunity to get to enough as you begin and go through your own process of downsizing. It can be painful; and it is the right thing to do.

At the beginning of most chapters is a saying, usually in the form of a question, that invites us to think about some aspect of the idea of "enough." These are from a boxed set of cards I wrote around the concept of enough. If you like the sayings and would like to have a box of cards for yourself or to give as a gift, please see my website signofenough.com. The cards can be ordered under the "Toolkit" tab. I would love to send you a box.

Also at the beginning of each chapter is a small symbol that looks a bit like an hourglass. As you can see on the title page, this is the symbol for Sign of Enough. It represents drawing the universal energy and the earth energy to our heart center, where we will find we are completely enough just the way we are.

Listening

*If you knew that it is exactly the right time for
you to begin the journey with the question
"How will I know when I have enough?"*

What would be your first step?

WHEN I FIRST STARTED thinking about this book, I
asked a friend "How does an author listen to a reader?" I realized that what I really want to do is to listen to you, my reader. I want to listen to your sadness, your distress, your
overwhelm. I want to listen to your fear, your longing, your
regret. I want to listen to you because I've been there; I've
been through it, and I know one of the most important things
that friends could do for me during that time was to just listen. I know what wasn't helpful. It wasn't helpful for people
to tell me, "Oh it's going to be just fine. You're really going to
like your new place." The following sentence is proudly dis-
played on the website of an organization that advertises itself
as offering a Senior-Friendly Guide to Downsizing: "Your
downsizing doesn't have to be stressful, sad, or scary. Stay
positive and get excited about a simpler life in a new place
with less clutter." I think that was written by someone who
has never been through a significant downsizing. That kind of

talk did me no good. That's not where I was, and I didn't want to hear it. What I wanted was just to be listened to so that I could talk from my heart about the pain I was feeling much of the time.

So, that's what I want to do. I want to listen to you. As you're reading, imagine that we're having a conversation and I'm listening to you as you're listening to me. And we'll go from there. I have no idea if this will work. All I know is that at this moment in time, there's nothing I want any more than for you to feel listened to. So, let's begin.

It is a very short book, and I suggest you read it all the way through, and then go back and do any of the exercises or fill in any of the lists that seem helpful to you in the moment. And if none of them seem helpful, just forget it and enjoy the conversation we've just had.

This book might be helpful for anyone wanting to let go of many of the things they have acquired over the years. It is particularly intended for those of us who are needing to do so not so much from choice as from necessity because it's come to that time in our lives[1] when we're leaving a place we may have lived for many, many years, and moving to a place that is significantly smaller. We may be leaving a place where we've lived with a spouse for many years, where we've raised several children, where we've cycled through many well-

---

[1] While writing this book, I talked to many people who had downsized, were in the middle of it, or were "getting ready to get ready." One of the things I found that, almost across the board, none of us thinks it is "that time" yet in our life. And whether we're 60 or 90, if we're still fairly healthy and able to get around, it seems too soon. The second thing I often heard was that if we wait until that time when we aren't so healthy and can't get around pretty well, it can be almost too late because it has become much, much harder.

loved pets. There may have been countless family gatherings, friends' dinners, birthday, anniversary, promotion celebrations. And in addition to the memories and paraphernalia associated with all that, we have an endless number of pictures capturing these deeply experienced occasions. In many of these pictures there probably are people we've loved, laughed and cried with who are no longer with us. Going through all this can be a very painful process. I hear you. I'm right here with you. Tell me all about it.

Introduction

ON A BEAUTIFUL EARLY SPRING MORNING I was sitting at my dining room table in my big house, ostensibly taking part in a writing course. It was time for a "writing segment," but I was looking around the room at all the things I needed to get rid of. How was I going to DO this? I mean emotionally, how was I going to get rid of 90% of what was in that room that I had collected over many years? There were so many books and treasured memorabilia in the bookcases. There was the clock that the love of my life had made for me years ago before he died. There was my piano, my banana chair from when I lived in the UK, the beautiful red-patterned Oriental rug that I'd always loved.

Not being able to stand that any longer, I looked outside. There I saw my beautiful white Buddha statue, all the pots and planters, the stylized bicycle planter that I'd so agonized over because of the inflated price. And this was only out the dining room window! I had a huge yard with a raised bed garden and a greenhouse where I could start the seeds in the late winter. There was my hot tub and the orange, apple, lemon, and lime trees, the blueberry bushes and the raspberry plants. On the patio were the fountain and the beautiful redwood table and chairs that in the summer held my very favorite bright red umbrella.

And on and on. And in that moment I understood a little better why I was having such difficulty figuring out what to do physically with all the stuff. I simply couldn't focus. It hurt too much to focus. Like many of us, I'd spent years trying to understand how I was feeling at any given moment, and now all I wanted was to *not* feel so I could get on with the sorting process.

If this sounds familiar, welcome to *The Upside of Downsizing: Getting to Enough*. This is not a "how to" book. There are plenty of people you can hire who will be more than happy to tell you how to go about downsizing. They'll even do lots of it for you for a fee. What this book will do for you, I hope, is make the whole process easier, not physically but emotionally. Not too long ago I heard a friend describe her image while she was downsizing as "taking it to the curb." For me the feeling was more like "kicking it to the curb." And that helped me crystalize why what I was doing felt so painful. It often times felt violent; a ripping me from things I loved. And in a strange way, when I could understand the process I was going through in that way, it actually became less painful. And when I was able to make the process less painful, I was able to make it more expeditious. I was able to get to enough, which made the whole ordeal go much more smoothly. So let's get started. What does it mean to downsize to enough?

Friends

*If you knew that courage begins to flow as you
take the first steps toward an important goal,
what would you begin?*

MY STRONG ADVICE before you begin any major downsizing and moving process is this: get yourself some really
good friends. The very first actual step I took toward what
would become a four-month downsizing process was accept-
ing my friend Lynn's offer to help me do whatever I needed
to get done on a chilly, cloudy Saturday afternoon. Now Lynn
is very budget- and value-conscious, which often is an extremely positive and valuable trait. But not when it comes to
helping someone downsize. Knowing this about her, I told
her that I would very much welcome her help; however, she
must encourage me to get rid of things and not try to get me
to see all the ways I might be able to use something in the
future.

With Lynn and others I quickly learned that the explana-
tion that worked best was this: "I had to make the decision to
get rid of this once. Please don't make me have to make it
again." See, the thing is, in most cases you acquired something because you thought it would be helpful, or useful, or
pretty or something. And that may still be true. But have you

used it? Have you used it enough to warrant its taking up some of your new, valuable, minimal space?

Anyway, she came and we began. The kitchen, actually, was a perfect place for me to start because I have less trouble getting rid of things in the kitchen than in any other room of the house. This will not be true for all of you, and especially not for those who are real cooks, which I am not. So, we got through most of the kitchen in one afternoon, and got rid of lots and lots of stuff. Now it's true that many bags of things went home with Lynn, but that's up to her — and I got it out of my kitchen.

Oh, that the whole process had been this easy. I hope it is for you; it certainly was not for me. As time went along it got more and more painful. But that's for later. At this point I was luxuriating in the feeling of opening up the cupboards, drawers and counter top so that my kitchen felt more spacious and much less crowded. I was getting to enough! It might be worth it to think of the place or places that you think will be easiest for you to clear out, and begin there so you have some "wins" and also keep your energy and spirits up.

One of the other times my friends were invaluable was during a garage sale I had after a month or so of downsizing. I had literally mountains of stuff in the driveway and at least as much still inside the house at the beginning of the morning. There is no way I could have handled that on my own. Lynn and her husband Steve came first, and then Martha came with some snacks, and then Corrine came with breakfast for us workers. We never stopped until late that afternoon, at which point they piled what was left in their cars and dropped it off at Goodwill on their way home. See what I mean about good friends? It was an exhausting day, and I made quite a bit of money. More importantly I got rid of lots and lots and lots of stuff, didn't have to pay anyone to haul it away, and kept it out of the landfill for at least a bit longer.

So, get yourself some friends, and decide where you think you're most going to need their help. Then when they say, "Let me know how I can help," you can quickly say, "Well, as a matter of fact, what I most need help with is..." whatever it is. Good friends want to help, but they're not going to know what to do unless you tell them.

1. What do you know right now you're going to want some help with?

2. Keep adding to this list as you think of things. Remember, people want to help, they just need to know what you'd like them to do.

Organize Me

*If you knew that it is OK to show as much
compassion toward yourself as you do toward others,
what would you begin to forgive yourself for?*

WHEN I MADE THE DECISION to downsize and move, I quickly realized I couldn't do it on my own. I was going from a four-bedroom house with a two-car garage and a big yard and garden full of stuff to a one bedroom apartment with a 46"x46" cage in the basement for storage. Obviously, this meant I needed to get rid of a huge amount of stuff. My real estate agents suggested I work with a downsizer, and gave me the names of two women I could interview. I already had met a woman at a downsizing seminar, so I prepared to talk with the three different women. And different they were!

Woman #1 was lovely, and I thought she would be delightful to have coffee with. I also suspected she'd let me get away with keeping lots of stuff when I claimed treasure after treasure. I knew that was not going to work. Woman #2 is, I suspect, a very good business woman. She has a big staff, and I'm sure they know how to get things done. I didn't feel, however, that she really listened to me, or understood how I was feeling and how I saw this move. For her, I think, I would have been a "project" and approached just like every other project she has. Woman #3, the woman I worked with for three months, really listened to me and seemed to understand how I was feeling about my upcoming move. And I had no doubt that she would not let me get away with keeping bunches of stuff I simply was not going to have room for.

As the saying goes, be careful what you ask for. Oh boy! Did I get what I had asked for! For three months, every Saturday and Sunday, we would march from room to room, drawer to drawer, closet to closet, where she would dump everything into a shallow box and I would go through the "Keep, Donate, Trash" routine. Very quickly the keep pile became two categories of Keep and Garage Sale. We also had boxes for paper recycle, plastic recycle and e-waste. And there was no messing around! We'd take a very short break for lunch, and sometime in the afternoon I would holler "Tea!" But other than those two breaks, we worked for hours and hours without even a pause. Makes me tired now just thinking about it. And there were many, many times when for the hundredth time she would say, "OK, now put that over there," and I really had to stop myself from saying "If you want that friggin' thing over there, put it there yourself!"

But the process worked. I had a huge and very successful garage sale, made lots of donations to good causes, and kept a small percentage of what I'd started out with.

Why do I tell you all this in a book I've said would not deal with the "how" of downsizing but only with the emotional part of it? I think it's important for each of us to have a realistic sense of the energy, stamina, and resolve it takes to successfully manage a large downsizing. The exhaustion exacerbates the sadness, the anger, the sense of loss, the fear of the unknown. And so it is very important for you to take good care of yourself during this process. What specifically do I mean by that? Well, all the obvious stuff like eat well, get lots of sleep, continue whatever exercise program you have, and drink lots of water. All of that is really important. I think, however, there are two other things that are even more important, and those are to stay in touch with your close friends, and to maintain or develop a meditation practice. Why do I highlight those two things?

I suspect the importance of "staying in touch with close friends" is fairly obvious. On the practical level, I simply could not have had a successful garage sale if several of my friends had not spent the entire day helping me and then filling their cars with all the stuff left over and taking it away. At that point in the day I was so emotionally and physically spent that I could not have done one more thing, including getting that left over stuff back inside the garage. And my good friend Lynn has spent many days helping me go through a second "cleansing" of some particularly troublesome places, like my office where I have the most trouble getting rid of things.

In line with this, did I mention that I'm not sure downsizing is ever done? I did an initial "purge" of all rooms, closets, cabinets, etc., with my downsizer. But later I looked back over some places, like the garage, and realized that even though I had eliminated lots and lots, I still had too much for the space I was moving into. So, a second culling was needed. And in each case where I've done this, the second time is harder than the first because even though I really like something or think it might be really helpful, or whatever, I simply may not have room for it. Period. So, you will need someone there to keep you going. If I hadn't had Lynn, I would just have sat down and had yet another cup of tea!

The second reason to stay in touch with close friends is support. I absolutely needed the emotional support that my friends consistently and tirelessly provided. I have several examples, but perhaps the most compelling is my friend and neighbor Maxine. She and her husband Ken absolutely did not want me to move. And yet knowing the reasons I made the decisions I did, she has been unfailingly supportive. And supportive in the best possible ways. Never once has she gushed about how much I'm going to love where I'm going when I get used to it. Nor has she ever said how everything is going to be just fine. She has always met me emotionally where I was and listened and listened and listened. She often agreed enthusiastically with me how absolutely shitty some particular event or person had been. And once I was able to get all that out, I felt much more positive, lighter, and able to get up and get on with it. And she did this almost daily.

I highlight good friends rather than partners and family because good friends tend to have "cleaner" motivation in their helping, and there are probably fewer years of "emotional baggage" with friends than with partners and family. This isn't always true, of course. Just a suggestion. I am reminded of the story a friend of mine told me. While she was helping her mother begin a fairly large downsizing, she overheard her mother say to a neighbor that, according to her daughter, she was doing it all wrong. Hrumph. See, better not to use family members, if possible.

And finally, we're going to talk about the importance of a meditation practice in Chapter 12, but for now let me just say that it will be very helpful if you have a "quick and easy" way to get back to your center, breathe, and let go of the accumulating stress.

The Garage Sale

FOUR WEEKS AFTER THE DOWNSIZING BEGAN, the day arrived for the GARAGE SALE. This was a big deal to me because both of my realtors and various and sundry others directly or peripherally involved in my downsizing project advised that garage sales didn't work any longer, that prospective buyers didn't come out as they used to do, that it usually was lots of work for very little money. In addition to all that, I knew I would come face-to-face with letting go of many things that had been important to me. But I needed to get rid of LOTS of stuff, and so I decided to go ahead.

If you make the same decision, absolutely positively get some "volunteers" to help. I had four good friends there, and we worked from early morning until late afternoon. My instructions to them were, "If somebody wants to buy it, sell it! Otherwise I will have to pay someone to come and take it away!" Generally speaking, this worked, but I know there were a handful of times when one of the "workers" just could not accept an offer of $2.00 for something in perfect condition that had cost many times that amount.

The hardest part for me was not the disparity between what something had cost and what was being offered. The hardest part for me was when something with deep sentimental value to me was involved. I remember two things in particular. The first were some braided wool rugs that my mother had made. When we cleaned out her house, I acquired several of these, and they were beautiful. And my mother had made them. And when I looked closely, I could see wool from some of the skirts I had worn in high school until they were too small or simply wore out. I didn't see when the last rug went, but I found myself silently pleading, "All the people who bought a rug, my mother made that rug. Please take good care of it and love it for me."

And then there was the admittedly strange-looking footstool. When someone asked, "What IS that?" I said "That is a footstool my father made." And I silently added, "So, please treat it with care, and experience the delight at the innovative design that foils everyone who sees it."

All in all it was a very, very hard day for me. I made lots and lots of money, and got rid of lots and lots of stuff. I absolutely, positively could not have done it without the help of my friends. No way. So, if you do hold a garage sale, be sure to enlist the help of some friends.

What astounded me with a little passage of time was that even though I had gotten rid of literally mountains of stuff, I didn't really miss anything. Isn't that amazing? Now, the same may not be true for you, but if it is, then I think we need to ponder the amount of stuff we actually don't need at all. Even if some of that stuff is very hard to part with. It's simply taking up space. Space we may need to clean periodically. Space we actually may be paying for. Filled space that may keep us "stuck" in all kinds of ways that we're not aware of.

And this brings us back to the question I've asked several times: "How will I know when I have enough?" It is so important that we live with this question and walk the path in getting to an answer because many of us are taking up more than our fair share of space. We're adding to the load of stuff that our beautiful planet is going to have to figure out how to deal with when we get rid of it. And as we acquire all that stuff, we're using up way more than our fair share of the earth's resources.

I tried to think about all this as I watched some of my precious stuff disappear that day for less than one-tenth of what it was worth. Sometimes that helped and sometimes it didn't. I don't know that anything really assuages the pain of parting with things that are precious to us even if they mean nothing to others. If you're feeling this, you are not alone. All of us who have gone through major downsizings have experienced the same thing, each in our own, individual way.

1. What are some of the things you think will be the hardest for you to part with? (For example, family heirlooms, pictures, things that were important to your children while they were growing up?) Make a list of these things:

2. Now, next to each thing or category of things, is there a person who might be happy to have them, or is there an organization that would welcome them as a donation? (For example, I gave hundreds of books to the local library that holds book sales as their primary fund raiser.)

3. And if you knew that each person or organization that you thought of did in fact receive the items, how do you think you would feel?

Things Disappearing

*If you knew that nothing outside yourself can
bring lasting fulfillment, what would you begin to
treasure deep inside yourself?*

BIT BY BIT, OR TRUCK LOAD BY TRUCK LOAD, things
are disappearing out of my house. This morning I watched
my wonderful, huge, white desk and cabinet disappear out
the door. I've had those for YEARS, and they have seen me
through so much. Yesterday I watched a beautiful antique
chest and a dining room table and four chairs disappear out
the other door. These were things my mother had lovingly
restored. Hours and hours of removing old paint and stain,
and more hours and hours of rubbing the new paste into the
wood. The table and chairs lived on our enclosed back porch
the entire time I was growing up. The table held all those
items that no one could decide what to do with, but that
might be needed for something, sometime. And then after the
restoring, the table and chairs sat proudly in my parent's
house until the day I couldn't stand to have them go into the
auction. So they lived in my house for a couple of years. And
now they're going to live in someone else's house who has no
idea of their history. When I told a friend about this, she said
that when she was selling and donating many things that had

belonged to her parents, she had the distinct feeling that she was dishonoring her mother and father. That's potent stuff! If this happens for you, it's really important to try to remember that this is just, for example, a table. That's all it is. And I'm saying this at least as much for me as for you, my precious reader.

On another day I watched my big old rocker and ottoman disappear out through the garage. It's true that those will be back, dressed in their spiffy new upholstery, but it still felt like another loss when it happened.

And that day while I ate my breakfast, I decided to start through some of the piles of pictures I need to get rid of. What I was struck by the most was an even deeper sense of loss than just throwing away the pictures. So many people who have been really important in my life are now dead. I have wonderful memories of them, but I don't have them.

I have to keep coming back over and over again to my core; the part that's really me; the part that, actually, is always whole and at peace. Some days that core is harder to find than other days, which is very strange because usually I feel incredibly grounded. Usually I can quiet myself by letting go of the tension around my eyes and in my shoulders, either closing my eyes or using "soft focus," and concentrating on the breathing in my belly. You may have your own way of finding your core. If you don't, I encourage you to spend some time discovering a way and then practicing it because it will serve you very well during the difficult days.

About this time someone asked me whether or not, as hard as this all is, I'm a little bit excited about where I'm going. I didn't miss even one nanosecond of a beat, and said, "No." When people ask you how you are, you don't need to make it up. You can just answer for real. They won't crumble, and you'll feel better for being honest.

1. How are you feeling right now about your current or upcoming downsizing? Be as honest and as specific as you can be.

Random Thoughts at Night

*If you knew that the only way you can honestly
feel compassion for others is to first feel compassion
for yourself, when would you begin
to soothe yourself?*

SUDDENLY AS WE GET CLOSER to putting the house on the market, everyone seems to feel more in charge of what's going on. The stager is ordering us all around. The real estate agent seems to acquiesce to her and to the gardener he hired to do some work outside.

Look folks, this is MY house, and I'll say what we are and what we aren't going to do. Got it?

I know when I start feeling this way, I can get really, really stubborn, which is not going to help the situation one bit. So I'm going to try to let it be known **I'm** in charge without having to be the biggest bully.

I am so tired. I am so tired. I am so tired. I wish I could go to sleep. Everything gets worse when it's dark. And late. And I know I need to go to sleep, but the thoughts and feelings won't stop.

I know that Bu, my cat, and I will be fine. I know Bu and I will be fine. I know Bu and I will be fine.

But then there's Mellie, my beloved cat for 14 years who lived and died in this house. How can I leave her? Mellie, will you please come with us? And there's the beautiful tree in the backyard. I planted that tree. He was a baby, so we put big poles next to him to keep him safe. He's a big, gorgeous California pine now. Please don't cut him down just to get more sun in the back yard. His name is Sammy, just in case you care.

It's so hard when person after person talks about all the things about the house, yard, furniture, pictures that are wrong, wrong, wrong, and DEFINITELY need to be fixed before the house can possibly be shown. I think it looks pretty good. I bought all the stuff inside and out, and I did things the way I did because I liked it that way. And I still do. So, just shut up.

During this time my mind is feeling as if it's not my own. I seem to be beset with upsetting, random thoughts that spring from nowhere. I don't know what the remedy for this is. All I know is that if you've been feeling this way, you are not alone. Right now I'm feeling more alone than I think I've ever felt in my life. And so I text my friend Shirley and ask for an electronic hug. And as I do that, I realize that clear through the years and years of my cancer surgery and treatment, I don't think I ever asked for a hug. This downsizing, friends, is very big stuff. Be gentle with yourself.

Sometimes we can feel very alone during the downsizing process. At times like this, different things help different people. Some examples might be contacting a friend, praying or meditating, going for a walk, listening to a particular piece of music.

1. What are some of these things for you?

Is My Stuff Part of Me?

If you stand quietly and look around
and say to yourself,
"I am enough right now," what changes for you?

IF ANYTHING BRINGS INTO SHARP FOCUS the question we ask ourselves when working with the Sign of Enough— "How will I know when I have enough?" —it is going through a huge downsizing. What I recommend to everyone, no matter how old you are, is to start getting rid of stuff now and live that way from now on. Some of us think that we'll save things so we can hand them along to our kids. From the people I talked to as I was writing this book, you might want to check that out with your kids, if that's what you're doing. Many people have found that their kids don't want any of the things their parents had been lovingly saving for them, sometimes for years. They don't want the beautiful bone china or priceless silver or elegant crystal. They don't want the gorgeous table linen. In fact, they don't want the table! And so far as stuff that belonged to them—the trophies, prom outfits, graduation tassels—they don't want that stuff, either... but they don't want you to throw it out. Any of this sound familiar? If so, it's time to just begin getting rid of things.

I am reminded of the conversation I had with someone who agreed to talk to me about his feelings as he and his wife were beginning a downsizing process. In looking through various storage areas of their house, they discovered that they had lots and lots of stuff that had belonged to their children as they were growing up. When asked, the now adult children wanted one small thing—they all wanted the same one small thing—a small rock that had been hand-painted with the image of a frog. They wanted nothing else, and suggested their parents take pictures of all that stuff before they got rid of it. The man I spoke with began to do that, until he realized it was a silly thing to do, and just stopped. And then got rid of all the stuff...except the frog.

Stuff, stuff, stuff. Last weekend at the garage sale the driveway was piled high with stuff and, as things sold, friends carried more stuff out from the piles in the house. I thought of those wonderful pictures in the book *Material World: A Global Family Portrait* by Menzel, Mann and Kennedy that show families around the world standing outside their abode with all the stuff they own piled around them. It's a strong reminder of how much "haves" have and how little "have nots" have. Anyway, I got rid of lots of stuff. And then dear friends piled their cars with unbought stuff and took it off for donation.

When everything was over, I walked back inside. In all honesty I could hardly tell that anything was gone. How sobering is that?

And yet...

The process of gathering things, selling things, bargaining with people whether something I paid quite a bit for should be sold for $2.00 or $2.50, and watching all that stuff go off with people I didn't know was very painful.

So, I've been thinking about all this quite a lot ever since the weekend. And what I think I find most amazing is this: I go shopping either to a store or online. I see something I want. I may or may not NEED it, but I want it, and so I buy it. I bring it home or it arrives. From the moment I hold it and look at it, it somehow becomes part of me. It's mine. And when it comes time to part with it, that action can feel "wrenching," especially if I don't really want to part with it or if it has been one of my favorite things in some way. And when is this feeling not so intense? For me it's when I am replacing the object with a shiny, new one.

I'm not talking about people and pets here. I'm talking about an inanimate object that we have bought and set down somewhere where it stayed until someone moved it. And I'm also not talking about those few things that, when we look at them, "spark joy," as described by Marie Kondo in *The Life-Changing Magic of Tidying Up*. I'm talking about all the rest of the stuff we have that is piled here and there, crowded into closets, drawers, attics, garages, external storage units that we pay a not insignificant amount for every month. It's all that stuff that still may cause us to cringe when we start to dispose of it. And THAT is what we need to explore.

Here are some questions that might help in that exploration:

1. When did your stuff become part of you? When you first got it, or after you had it for some time?

2. What kinds of stuff are the hardest for you to get rid of? Kitchen stuff? Office stuff? Clothes? Shoes? Sports equipment? Hobby tools, e.g. cameras, lenses, bags? Memorabilia? Gifts? Family treasures?

3. Who are you without all this stuff? What changes? Where in your body do you feel that loss?

4. How exactly does it feel to get rid of stuff that you really like, yet doesn't "spark joy" even though you don't intend to replace it?

No Longer A Decision-Maker, Apparently

If you knew that your core happiness depends up-
on your taking responsibility,
what would you become responsible for?

IF YOU'RE OLDER OR A WOMAN—and especially if you're an older woman—you may begin to notice that the realtor or someone operating in that capacity will begin to take over all decisions. Now, you may have been making all the major decisions regarding living successfully in this world for all or most of your adult years. And suddenly someone decides—unconsciously, I have to assume—that you're no longer capable of deciding anything!

This morning I wanted to get clarity from my realtor about the costs of painting, landscaping, staging, etc., that I had agreed to but I had not signed one single contract. He assured me it was irrelevant because they were people he and his partner had worked with for many years, that the costs would be deducted from escrow and, anyway, I could deduct the costs from my capital gains taxes when the time came.

This reminded me of the times I've been with a medical doctor and I blanched at how much something was going to cost. Many times the response I got was something like "You don't have to worry about this. Your insurance will pay."

I was extremely relieved that my insurance would pay that outrageous amount, AND that wasn't really the main issue. The main issue was that it was hugely overpriced and NO ONE should pay that amount. I said to my realtor that I still like to know what I'm paying for things.

My realtor is a very, very nice man, so I can only imagine what others in my situation may go through.

This is a reminder: YOU are in charge here, if you want to be. This is YOUR house, YOUR move, and YOUR life. Others are, thankfully, facilitating the downsizing and the move, but all the decisions are yours, with advice from them, of course, but you're still in charge. Don't give that up unless you choose to. I think this is so important because during the process of downsizing, moving, etc., we are in many ways losing our roots; roots we may have had for many, many years. For me it becomes so important to hold on firmly to who I am; to go right to the center of my being and tell myself clearly and concisely "I am me, and I am enough, just the way I am," and not to let anyone—anyone I've hired, any friends, or even any well-meaning family member—take that away. This highlights one of the reasons it is important to begin to take "downsizing action" earlier rather than later. Generally speaking, the younger and more vibrant you are, the easier it will be to retain control during the downsizing and moving process. So, if you're thinking that you're going to need to do this "soon," START NOW!!

I spoke with several people professionally involved with helping people downsize and move, and across the board they said that the earlier people begin, the better. It takes a huge amount of energy and stamina to get through this successfully, and it can become just "too late." It can come to the point that the ordeal is simply more than someone can deal with. And it certainly can come to a time when you no longer will have the oomph to stand up for yourself and retain control of what happens to all your precious possessions.

1. Whom do you find it hardest to stand up to during your downsizing process (or if you haven't begun yet, whom do you imagine this might be?) This could be one or several different people, and it could change during the process.

2. Think now what you might say to these people so you don't regret what you say when the time comes, and yet you remain strong and firm.

Is This Nirvana?

From *A Life* by Zbigniew Herbert:

I know
it's hard to be reconciled
not everything is exactly
the way it ought to be

but please turn around
and step into the future
leave memories behind
enter the land of hope

THIS MORNING I TRIED to get into these words of Herbert, and just couldn't. Sometimes looking to the future where everything will be "just fine" is just not possible. You know the feeling.

Every day this week when I got home I found my house wrapped in plastic so they could power wash the eaves. The first day was a shock, and I ran around ripping holes where the windows are so I could get some air for me and my cat. But as we've learned, one can get used to anything. So, after the first day I just sighed and looked for which door they had left unwrapped so I could get in. THIS IS MY HOUSE, GUYS!

I'M LIVING HERE! Can people get too focused on their work, missing what the impact will be on others? Or is it that they're not focusing at all, but just doing?

Anyway, that was some of this week. Nevertheless, I did learn an important lesson somewhere along the way, which usually happens if I will just pay attention.

What I learned is this: Hearing someone say, "Everything is going to be just fine! You're going to love it in your new place!" is NOT helpful right now. Just as Herbert's poem is not helpful right now. But what <u>was</u> helpful was a different kind of reality check. A notice arrived from the bank telling me what my new mortgage payment would be in several months. Gulp. I was so relieved that I wouldn't have to be paying that. I could afford it, at least for a while, but why use my resources that I've worked so hard for that way? What I want to do is to keep doing the work I love, travel to see new places and people, travel to see people I've known for a long time and love lots and lots. I want to go to the symphony, the opera, the theatre. I want to buy all the books I want. I want to go out to eat with friends, and I want to be able to take them out for their birthday. I want to continue to live my life as much as possible just exactly the way I am doing now. I don't want all my resources going into the place I live. Big "ah hah" moment for me.

A second helpful reality check was realizing that I don't, actually, live in Nirvana now. I love the house, the yard, the neighborhood, and the neighbors. In fact I wanted a house like this my whole life; windows everywhere, doors to the outside in almost every room, huge backyard with a garden. And yet, there are some "big ticket" items that will come due in the next year or two: the house will need to be repainted;

the roof will need to have major repairs or be replaced; some of the siding on the house will need to be repaired, and who knows what's underneath. There are growing parking problems in the neighborhoods since there are more and more of us in the world with more cars per family than at any other time in history. All the services from the city are more expensive for homeowners every year. The property tax keeps going up. And on and on and on. As I get older, I get more wary of all this. I hate it, and I worry about taking care of the house and yard and garden on a day-to-day basis.

So, all *this* is the kind of "reality check" that helps. At least a bit.

I invite you, when you're ready, to make this kind of assessment. There certainly are lots of things you love about where you are and may have been for many, many years.

And now look at the ways in which it is not perfect. In fact, there may be issues that you have growing concerns about and have just not wanted to face. Is there maintenance that you've kept putting off because it is potentially very expensive or disruptive? Are there changes in the neighborhood that you're not excited about? Have daily "chores" around the house and yard become a little daunting? Overall, would you just like for things to be a little easier? You will have your own list; this is mine and won't necessarily ring true for you. For me, doing this was a helpful reality check. I hope it is for you, too.

1. You probably know the things you love about where you live right now. Just to make a more complete picture of reality, list all of the things about the house/apartment/condo that aren't wonderful.

2. Include everything in the surrounding area that may not be terrific.

Feeling Empty

*As you look around, everything in the natural
world is a gift.*

*As you reflect on this, what do you feel most
grateful for?*

A FRIEND OF MINE ASKED ME the other day how I was feeling. That sounds like a pretty easy, straightforward question; however, I found it hard to answer quickly. I mean, I could have said "Just fine! How are you?" But I was pretty sure that's not what she meant. She wasn't asking me that as a substitute for "Hiya," as we often actually mean when we say, "How ya doin'?"

As I thought about it, looking for an answer, what I realized was that I felt close to absolutely nothing! What it most reminded me of was that feeling I have when I get off a really long flight. It's that sense of being hollow, having nothing "in there" where the real, deep me resides. One time when I was feeling this way, I realized that it felt as if my body was here standing in my living room and my soul, my essence, was still somewhere over the Atlantic, and it was going to take some time for it to catch up with the rest of me. In this case, however, I couldn't figure out where my soul was... it was just gone. I wondered when it would come back? I was almost glad it was gone. I was sure it was somewhere taking care of itself, and, therefore, taking care of me. I haven't had a major meltdown; I haven't gotten sick even though many people around me have been coughing and sneezing for some time now; I've been "snippy," but, to my knowledge, I haven't lost any friends. So, thank you, soul. Just stay wherever you're hiding for a bit longer.

And I've even sort of gotten used to this gnawed-out feeling. I mean, I think we can get used to a whole lot that's not exactly pleasant. My house has been "staged" all week. In case you live somewhere that this isn't a common practice, what it means is that a "staging company" comes into your house and makes it look as if no one is now, or ever has, actually lived there. What it means for me at the moment is that my house can be shown every day between 9:00 AM and 6:00 PM, which means I have to be out of the house during those hours. It also means that when I look around, what I see is my furniture, and lots of someone else's crappy, cheap stuff. Stuff that looks as if it was acquired from some discount house that was going out of business. Fancy stuff, glitzy stuff, stuff that "smells good" to someone, I guess, but not to me. I sneeze.

I have a box in the closet in my bedroom. One in the coat closet off the living room. And two in the garage for the kitchen. When I get home from work, I go from box to box, putting me and my cat back into our house: his scratching pad, my toiletries, kitchen kettle, paper towels, pillows for the couch that I can actually lean against. And then every morning, the process reverses. And I've gotten used to doing this! I've gotten used to the glitzy crap, distributing my stuff around the house after work, and doing the reverse in the morning. But I haven't gotten used to the stinky, sweet smell.

I once learned that our sense of smell is one of our earliest, and therefore, most basic senses. Apparently, being able to find that nipple depends on smelling the milk that's inside.

Anyway, that's the routine I've become accustomed to, and it sort of freaks me out that I have. And I don't think I could have if my soul were still around.

As you probably can hear by now, the one feeling I do have is anger. I spend a great deal of time right now being really, really mad... at what? Often anything or body that's close at hand. And, as I said, to my knowledge I haven't lost any friends, which says mountains about my friends.

1. So, is what I've just described at all familiar to you? Have you had any of these feelings? If so, what words would you use to more closely describe what all this feels like to you?

2. If it's not at all familiar, how would you describe what you are going through? I'm assuming it's not been easy, but maybe it has, and that would be wonderful!

No Need To Worry

If you knew that the most important choice you
can make is about how you will live your life,
what changes might you make?

I'M SITTING IN MY FAVORITE COFFEE SHOP trying desperately to write something coherent. I've lived in my staged home a week and a half. The open house was this past weekend. Now we're waiting to see if any offers come in. If they do, we'll meet this afternoon and review them. And if they don't, I continue to live in my staged house and have an open house again this coming weekend, I assume.

A piece of advice: don't build your expectations on what your friends have said about whether or not you'll get good offers. Everyone I know said that the house would sell for way over the asking price and sell very, very quickly. Well, it's now several days after the open house, and we're still waiting to see if ANY offers come in. I knew I should be wary of what everyone was saying because selling a house is very fluky, but I find myself extremely deflated at the moment.

Realizing all this yesterday, I've tried to get into the mood of knowing it will all turn out very, very well. That what I really want is a win for everybody: a good outcome for me, very happy new owners who love the house and yard and so will take good care of everything, and happy neighbors because the new owners are such nice people. And it's absolutely true, that IS what I want. I just want it now. And then I try to clearly remember that it doesn't help me to continue to try to push the world around so things happen exactly the way I want them to. As His Holiness the Dalai Lama has said, "If a problem is fixable, if a situation is such that you can do something about it, then there is no need to worry. If it's not fixable, then there is no help in worrying. There is no benefit in worrying whatsoever." In this situation, I have done everything I can do. And since there is nothing else I can do, it does me absolutely no good to continue to worry about it. Right? Yep, that's right. Now, all I need to do is live that way. Easier said than done, isn't it?

All this comes back again, I think, to the feeling of having absolutely no control over something that is affecting my life so much. This is MY house that I've lived in for many, many years and loved. I have thousands of memories in this house. Now its fate and, in a very strong sense, my fate, is dangling somewhere out there, and there's absolutely nothing I can do but wait. Most of us like to feel "in control," even in the face of the reality that we actually control very, very little. We still hold the illusion that we're in control.

And now in this particular downsizing situation, time and time again, I have my face shoved into the reality that there is NOTHING I can do to make any impact on the decisions that others are going to make. Nothing, except continue to put my things away in the morning, wipe down all the surfaces, leave before 9:00 and not return until 6:00.

1. If at any point you begin feeling a complete loss of control to others, what is ONE thing you can identify that you <u>can</u> do?

2. And now can you think of just one more thing?

So Judgment Weary

If you knew that you can choose to feel complete
sufficiency,
what would be your next step?

OK. ONE OFFER CAME IN, and it was not at all attractive. So, when I left home this morning, again, I spent about 45 minutes putting all my things away and wiping down all the surfaces. And we'll have an open house again this coming Saturday and Sunday. Sigh.

What I'm feeling at this particular moment is very re-signed. And that is a lousy feeling. I much prefer anger and even frustration because there's some energy in those.

Resigned is just blah. And this is very hard for me. I am, generally, quite a happy, even-keeled person. But this down-sizing, staging, and total uncertainty about the immediate future is really getting to me. And I can add to that judgment because I have done lots of meditation, and I think I should be able to "do better" with the current situation. Isn't it amazing how we add to our woes by getting even more judgmental about ourselves?

I think I'm "judgment weary." From the very first walk-through my real estate agents did, I feel as if I've been mired in judgment. That visit involved a litany of everything that was wrong with my house—inside and out. Then the downsizer came, and week after week it was the same thing: "Why do you have all of this stuff? These things are so old; why do you keep them?" And on and on. When the various workers arrived outside, it seemed that no matter where they went something needed to be repaired, painted or removed. The final straw, of course, was the stager who clearly didn't like anything that was on any surface in my house. (We did keep most of my furniture because I insisted on a "partial" staging.)

All this became very hard to hear! This is MY house, which I love. These are MY things that I've selected, placed, and kept there. If I didn't like things the way they are, I would have changed them! At one point one of my real estate agents said "This needs to be fixed," and I said "Oh, it doesn't really bother me," and he said "The point isn't whether or not it bothers you. What matters is that it bothers me."

And he is one of the nicest men in the world. I can't imagine what it must be like to work with lots of the agents out there. I'm pretty sure it doesn't help to just "suck it up" and get on with it. Having been through weeks of anger and frustration, I know that doesn't help either. What helps? I'll have to let you know when I do, but this is what I know for now:

1. To the extent you can, before you begin the process of downsizing and moving from where you live now, decide how much you want to be involved in all the decisions that will need to be made. These include what things to keep and what things to get rid of. For the things you're getting rid of, what to sell and how (e.g., do you want to have a garage sale?), what to donate and where. Some people want to be very involved in all those decisions, and some people don't, and there's no right answer except what's right for you.

2. Again, right from the beginning, make how much you want to be involved very clear to all those helping you, whether they are people you've hired or they're family or friends.

3. Be prepared to remind people of what you want frequently, if necessary. Unless, of course, you change your mind along the way which is fine! You just need to make that known.

4. Whatever your decision about the level of your involvement, be consistent so the other people involved don't get confused.

This is Fear

If you knew that it is OK to show as much com-
passion toward yourself as you do toward others,
what would be your first steps toward taking better
care of yourself?

NOT BEING ABLE TO SLEEP last night, I tried to figure
out what was going on. When I really looked, it wasn't too
tricky. I was feeling really, really scared. That deep kind of
scared that I felt when I was a little girl and my mother would
have to get up out of her bed and come to sleep on the end of
mine. And the moment she arrived and got settled in, I was
fine and went to sleep. To get her there often meant many,
many minutes of my calling, first softly and, much to my sis-
ter's displeasure as she tried to sleep in the bed next to mine,
then louder and louder and louder: "Mommy. Mommy.
MOMMY. MOMMY. MOMMY!!!! <u>MOMMEEE</u>!!!!" Until she
finally woke up and came in.

And I realized THAT was exactly the level of fear I was
feeling. I had already gotten rid of so much of what I had
owned, my house was on the market, but hadn't sold yet, and
I had no idea what was going to happen next. And more importantly, I felt completely helpless and alone. Everything is
so much worse at night, isn't it?

For any of you who understand the chakra system, someone recently told me they thought I was working with first chakra stuff because it's about my grounding and stability. And I agree with them. What I thought about this morning when I was looking at the depth of my fear last night was, from the perspective of Maslow's Hierarchy of Needs theory, I'm not feeling at all safe. Safety is the need we have that is just above our physiological needs for things like food, water, warmth and rest. For many of us in modern Western society—although by no means all of us—it is fairly straightforward how to satisfy our safety needs, which might include such things as getting a place to live, having employment or some way to support ourselves, gathering a family, and so forth. But even when we have enough of these things and are not functioning at the "safety" level, none of them are by any means guaranteed to last. So, the reality of our human life is that we are not blissfully and permanently safe. We just trick ourselves into believing that we are because the reality that we're not is too frightening. And when we come face-to-face with not having some of our safety needs met, many of us have very little practice dealing with that fear. I suddenly just thought of that fatuous statement that someone will pull out to say to us all too often when we're going through a hard time, "What a fabulous learning experience!" Just makes one want to vomit, doesn't it?

So, what is the answer? I have no idea what THE answer is, but one answer I know from my meditation practice is that if I try to get away from pain or fear or discomfort, it just grows bigger and bigger and bigger. The only possibly successful thing to do is to go right into the middle of that difficult feeling and stay there until it changes in some way. Which it will. I've watched it many, many times. Several years ago I was diagnosed with a potentially life-threatening cancer. I'll never forget the day I was driving down the street and was absolutely drenched in fear. I almost had to pull over, and probably should have because I couldn't see very well. When I was able to tell myself, "OK Sara. This is just fear. It's only fear," and go right into it, it changed, and I could keep going.

What might this mean for you? Well, I hope in your downsizing and moving process you never experience this level of fear. But just in case...

I honestly don't think I could get through some of the times in my life if I didn't have an ongoing and fairly serious meditation practice. Recently I was interviewing a friend about all her experiences with helping family members downsize, and then her own experience of going from a 3000-square-foot house to a small, one bedroom one. When I asked her what advice she would give to someone who was going to need to downsize, she said that she thought the most important advice she would give is to develop a meditation practice. I was very surprised because I had never said that to her.

So, at a minimum it can't hurt and maybe it will help. There are many, many opportunities to learn how to meditate now. One of the most readily available in most places is Mind Body Stress Relief (MBSR) developed by Jon Kabat-Zinn at MIT Medical School. There are literally thousands of practitioners around the world, so just Google it until you find a course or workshop near you.

And for myself? I'm just going to try to remember to go directly into the fear when it arises because I deeply know that nothing else will really work. This is not a "logical" fear and, therefore, simply cannot be thought through or away. There probably are many ways to approach this kind of fear or whatever strong feeling you are experiencing. Using fear as the example, this is what I do:

1. Get very, very quiet. No matter what is going on around you, close your eyes if you can, and get very quiet. Breathe.

2. To the extent possible, name the feeling you're experiencing, for example, "This is fear."

3. Put your internal focus right into the center of that fear.

4. Keep your focus there until you can feel the fear begin to change. It's possible when you first focus on it, the fear will get bigger. Stay right with it until it lessens and then perhaps goes away. It will if you just stay with it.

The Land of the Waiting

*If you knew that when you are open hearted and
open handed it takes less effort to remain grateful for
what you have, what would you open to today?*

TODAY I'M IN THE LAND OF THE WAITING. I didn't
want to put my house up for sale, I didn't want to get rid of at
least half of what I owned, I didn't want to pay lots of money
to people to "spruce up" my house and yard, and then "stage"
it with stuff I don't like. I didn't want to sell my house. I
wanted NONE of what I've been doing to get ready for the
BIG EVENT: moving. But now that I've been through so
much of that, I'M READY to get on with it. I know people are
occasionally going in to look at my house. I know this because
either their real estate agent calls first to see if it's OK, or,
when I get home from work, I see that an agent has left a
business card. But I have no idea what the outcome is of any
of these "look sees."

And I'm fascinated that I haven't called my realtor to find
out. Me, Ms. Curiosity to the nth degree! And why haven't I? I
think it's pretty simple, really. I just don't want to know that,

so far as they know, there are no offers coming in this week. Aarrrugh!

I have literally dozens of stories about what is happening. There are two primary ones: #1 is that there are possibilities, and they don't want to tell me until they know for sure; #2 is that they know of no possibilities, and they don't want to give me that information. And then I have to remind myself that since, actually, I am not the center of everyone's universe, they may be busy doing other things and simply haven't focused on my house yet this week. After all, it's only Tuesday morning.

One of the things I've noticed during the past four months (FOUR MONTHS! That's a third of a year!), is that so many of my feelings and much of my behavior are completely atypical for me. How to explain that? For one thing, I think many of us are very different when we're under significant stress, which I feel I have been. But when we're under stress, are we different or are we "more so?" I know I inherited the "worry gene" from my Mother, whom I have described as an Olympic-level worrier. And now I can see that I'm right up there on the podium with her. So, maybe I do sort of worry much of the time, and maybe I'm not really as happy as I appear, and maybe I stifle my "snippiness" with people because I don't want to see myself that way. I don't know yet. I'll have to let you know when things are back to "normal."

Normal. Are things ever going to be normal again? When I was going through my cancer treatment, I remember several times all I wanted was for things to go back to normal. Back to before the diagnosis. Before the surgery and endless treatment. Before I was bald and tired and "chemo-brained." And I remember that it was easier when I took in the fact that things would never be "before cancer" again. THIS was the new normal. All this reminded me of a wonderful book by Anne Tyler titled *The Accidental Tourist*. It's a story about a man at very loose ends in his life who writes books for those who hate to travel. His advice is to make wherever you are as much like home as possible. This, also, of course, is a perfect recipe for making yourself miserable since the only thing that is exactly like home is home!

And so I go back to what my hair dresser said to me last week: "For God's sake, Sara. You have a house in Palo Alto. It's going to sell." Right, Michele. And after it does, I will get on with the new normal.

1. Can you remember any times when you just wanted things to get back to "normal?"

2. Did they, or did they go on to a "new normal?"

3. After a major change or significant event in our lives, can we ever get back to "normal?" Why or why not?

I'm Tired

Many of us spend the first 2/3 of our lives acquiring things and the last 1/3 of our lives getting rid of things. If this is true for you, when might you pause in acquiring?

I realized this morning I'm so tired. Bone deep tired. When I wake up after what I think has been a good night's sleep, I'm just not sure I can get out of bed and get on with it. And one of the things that ultimately gets me up is that I signed a form saying realtors could come into my house for showings at any time between 9:00 AM and 6:00 PM. Now THAT would be embarrassing! "Oh hello. I'll be up and dressed in just a minute. You'll love the house!" And I'm having increasing trouble sitting for any length of time at all because a spot in my tush gets so sore I have to stand up; and then it's hard to walk until I get going. I take this as a not-so-subtle reminder of how much of a pain in the ass all this has become. I started downsizing four months ago. I've been living in a staged house for going on four weeks. Really, it's time to get on with this.

This reminds me of something else that's important, I think. To the extent possible, it's really important to keep your sense of humor through all this. There is something ironically amusing about the fact that many of us spend two-thirds or our lives acquiring things, and the last one-third getting rid of them. What if we lived in exactly the amount of space we really need, and did not rent additional storage space? I'm getting ready to move from a 1610-square foot house with a double-car garage on a 9536-square foot property. Me and a cat. And I'm going to an 827-square foot apartment with a 46"x46" cage in the basement for storage. I decided not to spend more money and get a two-bedroom apartment because I really don't need the additional space. I love to have house guests. And I have them maybe twice a year. That's a lot of additional money every month per house guest! I'm reminded again of the book *Material World: A Global Family Portrait* with pictures of families around the world standing outside their abode. My new abode is way big enough for me.

Thinking about all this within a larger context doesn't necessarily make me feel better in the moment, but it does add a dose of reality to my current situation. And it does make me at least fleetingly more eager to be living in the amount of space I really need with the stuff I need on a day-to-day basis to live a very happy and fulfilling life. There is a good feeling that goes along with knowing I'm not taking up lots more space than 80% of the rest of the world's population has for an entire family; extended family in many cases. That does feel good. I think I'll try to stick with that for a while.

What are some other things I might try? I remember when I used to go backpacking and might be out for an entire week with only the things I could carry on my back. These were some of the happiest moments of my life. I'm also aware that there are times I've felt "crowded" by all my stuff and longed for more empty spaces. I think of the homeless people I've seen pushing one or more overflowing grocery carts with all their possessions dribbling out around the corners. In addition to feeling pangs of sorrow for them, I couldn't help but think how tied down they must be, having to keep track of and move all that stuff from place to place.

It's certainly true that many people don't have what they need. And there are many of us who have way more. Maybe learning how to live with less is going to feel good.

Saint Who?

*If you knew that each of us is really just passing
through,
what, if anything, would you want to leave behind
you?*

I COULD FEEL MYSELF GETTING PRETTY DESPERATE
and discouraged last week. My house had been on the market
for over a month, and in this market houses typically sell in
seven days or less. All my friends were absolutely incredu-
lous, not being able to understand why this beautiful house
with an absolutely huge yard was not selling. But it wasn't,
and I was tired of hearing my real estate agents tell me about
all the negative comments they were receiving about the
house. Sigh.

On Thursday a friend told me the story of selling her
mother's house. It had been on the market a long time and
was getting no offers. Katie said that she went out and bought
a small statue of Saint Joseph and buried him upside down in
her mother's yard, and the house sold right away.

Now, Katie described her mother as a very, very good
Catholic. Hmmmmm. So, I told Katie that I was not Catholic,

let alone a very, very good one. And she said "Sara! He's a Saint! He's been canonized! He's not prejudiced!"

OK then, I'm willing to try anything at this point. Where do I get a statue of Saint Joseph? Katie said I could get him at a Catholic store. I allowed as how there could be a Catholic store on every corner in the city where I live, and I would never have seen them. So, I Googled "Catholic store," adding my zip code. I tell you they are everywhere! The closest one was in a city between my office and my home, so that seemed like a good location. I called, and in a very quiet, embarrassed voice asked if they had small statues of Saint Joseph that you bury in the yard if you want to sell your house. The woman on the phone enthusiastically assured me that they did. So, well, OK! And then I thought about going there. I like that city, but it's very difficult to drive around in. So, what do we do in the 21st century when we don't want to go to a store? Right. I searched Amazon. And there was at least one whole page of little Josephs in small boxes that included instructions for burying! Who knew? By now it's Thursday night, and I'm having my fourth weekend of open house beginning Saturday afternoon. I need St. Joe now! So I paid extra for next day delivery.

When I got home from work Friday night, I excitedly went to the front door looking for the box from Amazon. No box. Oh no! I checked my email, and there was an email from earlier in the day saying the package had been delivered and was on the "back porch."

There is absolutely nothing at my house that anyone ever would describe as a "back porch." I fussed and fumed, and then I decided that since I spend literally hundreds of dollars on Amazon every year (I even buy my underwear there now!), it was NOT OK that this happened. I got a very nice young man at Amazon Customer Service who patiently listened to my tale of woe. And then he suggested that I wait until the next day to see if it showed up. And I asked, not unreasonably I thought, that if it has not been delivered, why did I get an email saying it had been? He paused a moment, and then said "we're working on that." Anyway, I whined long enough that he finally agreed to give me a full refund, including the extra I'd paid for shipping. Very good.

Except I still did not have my Saint Joseph for the next day's open house. First thing in the morning I drove to the Catholic bookstore. I really, really wanted to just find the little St. Joseph boxes rather than have to ask for them. But I couldn't find them. I approached one of the nuns behind the counter and quietly asked for what I wanted. "Oh yes," she replied, "right over here." And she took me to a bin of small, white, plastic Saint Josephs. No box. No instructions. Well, I knew from reading about it on Amazon what I was supposed to do. Then she said, "And you need the Novenas." I had no idea what she was talking about, but if she said I needed them, I wanted them. She handed me a small booklet that had what seemed to me to be prayers inside. I thanked her, bought my Joseph and his Novenas and drove home, also buying a couple of small Saint Joseph medals just for good measure.

By the time I got there, it was minutes away from when the open house would begin, and I was frantic to get St. Joe buried, only to remember I'd sold all my trowels! Oh yikes! So I went in the garage and found a strip of metal and began madly digging a hole right under the "For Sale" sign. In went Joseph, head first, and I got him all covered up. Not having the booklet of Novenas with me at that moment, I gave Saint

Joseph a Buddhist blessing. Katie said he wasn't prejudiced, and that's all I had right then. I learned that Novena has to do with the number nine, and I was to recite a Novena for nine days. OK man, I'm in.

I walked to the window from where I could see Joseph's spot every morning and every night, recited the Novena, and on the fourth day we got an offer. On the fifth day we got another one, and this one was really good. I accepted that offer, and the deal was closed on the fifth day. Out of respect I'm continuing to offer the Novena to Saint Joseph for the next four days. Thank you Saint Joseph.

I can understand anyone feeling skeptical about this. But I'm just saying... for an entire month I had received one not-very-good offer that was later withdrawn. On the fifth day after I buried Saint Joseph, I got a really good offer that I could happily accept.

Want to sell your house? Go get a Saint Joseph. You don't have to be a good Catholic, but, who knows? Maybe it helps if you are.

Oh, one final note, if you do that, you're supposed to dig him up and take him with you to your new place and put him in a place of honor. I will certainly do that.

Let It Flow

We all know, actually, that complete safety is not possible.
So, if you knew that you are safe enough, what would you attempt?

THERE ARE SEVERAL THINGS I BELIEVE that you may not, but stick with me if you can. I believe that we are largely made up of energy and that it flows around and through us all the time unless we do something, consciously or unconsciously, to stop it. (And when it's totally stopped, we die.) I believe we have some degree of control over that process, and so we can change it if we become aware of it and we want to make a change. I believe that at least some of this is "directed" by the human mind, of which we understand about .02% at the moment (my estimate). But some time we'll know more. Lots more. Just like all those enlightened beings who came before us and are with us right now. Some of whom we pay little attention to because we call them "crazy" or "way out" or too "woo woo."

With all that said, about the same time I heard of Saint Joseph, I had become convinced that one of the reasons my house was not selling was that I, actually, didn't want it to.

Well, that's not quite accurate. I was at the point of wanting it to sell, but I had not come to the point of wanting to move, to leave my house. And I told that to my friend Maxine. I said that I had the sense that the energy around the house was really, really stuck. I said that I had realized that if I'm honest, I still do not want to move, even though I've been "moving" in that direction for months and months. I thought of a conversation I'd had that day with my friend Amy. She had asked me when I'd said pretty much the same thing to her to say again what my larger goals were. What are the larger reasons for selling the house? I said to be more financially secure, to be able to stay in this area so I can continue to live pretty much the way I am living now for as long as I can, to simply be able to be happy and stop taking all of this so seriously. And both the conversations with Maxine and with Amy felt really good.

So, I went home and stood in the middle of my lovely, loved house. And I said "I feel as if we're stuck. And I feel as if it's time for both of us to move on." I could feel the house agree. And so I asked "Are you really ready now? Are you ready to move along and welcome the new people who will live here? Your mission in this lifetime of yours is to heal people. You healed me. Someone else now needs you. Can we go ahead?" And, finally, the house said *"Yes."* And I said "I will always remember you as my Healing Home." And the house said to me, *"And I'll always remember you as my Sunshine Girl."* And then we were free, open; our energy was flowing. We were both ready. Finally. And the house sold very soon after that. Timing? Energy? St. Joseph? Who knows!

Now I know this sounds really kinky to many of you. That's OK. You believe whatever you believe, and that's fine with me. But if you're having trouble moving ahead with what you know is next for you, then I invite you to examine what in you is holding you back. Are you sad? That's totally understandable. Are you afraid? That's totally understandable, too. Are there aspects of the "next step" that you resist? For me, I'm resisting the realization that I'm going to a retirement community. I'm going about 10-15 years before I would, I imagine, "naturally" want to go. And I stop when I hear myself say that. Are we ever "naturally ready" to make the huge kinds of changes the massive downsizing, packing, moving, beginning again in an unknown place with unknown people are calling for? I don't think many of us are. And so I think we need to be as clear as we can be about how we deeply are feeling about the whole next step. Recognize all those feelings. Honor them. They are very, very real, and totally understandable. And then take the next step even with all those feelings. As you take the next step and then the next and then the next, these feelings will very gradually diminish as they see that you are still just fine. Maybe not "delighted," but basically just fine. It's time.

It may take some time to answer these questions, so be patient with yourself:

1. Is there anything you're holding onto that you really need to let go of?

2. If so, is there something you can say or do that will help you let go?

Is There An End?

*Some of our desires are "healthy" and draw us in-
to happiness, joy and gratitude.
And some do the opposite. Which desires are most
present for you today?*

AT SOME POINT you get done with your downsizing. Or do you? I worked with my "downsizing woman" for about three months. And then I realized I hadn't done the "black hole" kitchen drawer. Do you have one of those? Well, I have to hold down the contents as I attempt to slide the drawer closed. And so when my friend Lynn offered to come over one day to help, I took her up on it.

Does anyone know why we save maybe 479 rubber bands? Innumerable picture hangers all missing half of what we'd need to hang a picture? Loose batteries that aren't dated, so who knows if they're still good, even though a piece of cardboard with nothing attached says that, apparently, at one point in time it had a battery tester. Various and sundry "thingies" that no one has any idea what to do with. Enough pens and pencils to equip at least one large grade-school classroom. And on and on. And yet...

It's incredibly hard to get rid of this stuff because who knows when I might need it? I know when I will need it. The moment the trash collector takes it away in the black bin. At that exact moment I will remember why I need that metal thingy with the bright red plastic corners. So, it was very helpful to have Lynn there, except what we found was that many of my unneeded items went home with her, just in case she might need them.

From the "black hole" drawer, we moved on to the big plastic bin that holds all the items I might need when I travel, including maybe 20 little cans of hairspray. The perfect travel size that they stopped making. I bought up the entire stock of a store where I found some. And then several months later they started making that size again. But I'm ready. Boy am I ready. I can't get rid of them just in case they halt production again.

Whew, NOW I'm done downsizing. Except this week I realized I wasn't. I still needed to do the drawers and cubby in the guest bathroom. I have no idea what's there. That's how much I use the stuff.

So, there seems to be always yet one more place I forgot about. I suppose this will end when the packers find the totally forgotten about places.

There are also the places I have gone through, in some cases ruthlessly, that I realize still need a more thorough "scrubbing," like the closet in my office. Yes, padded mailers are important. And I will need that box of 1000 mailers only when my products are wildly desired in the popular market. So, even though I think I've gone through every nook and cranny, there are several places that need a redo. Just like that closet. And like the garage, which my friend Lynn casually noted looked as full as it always had. Aaarugh! I've decided downsizing is like taking care of an older house. One is never really done. With downsizing, it is done the day you move... or is it?

(I later realized I needed to get rid of lots more stuff when I completely ran out of storage space in my new apartment.)

What Ground?

If you get very still and listen to your heart, you
will hear it whispering to you
"You are enough... just exactly the way you are."

A VERY STRANGE THING HAPPENED this week. Something I had never experienced before. I had just spoken to my real estate agent. During that conversation I learned that he is leaving for an extended vacation next week and won't be around for the actual close of escrow. I learned that on Friday of this current week I will go to the title office and sign off on all the final papers for selling my house. Then on the day escrow does close, my agent's father will call to say the closing has occurred. I know this man very well; in fact, I knew him before I knew his son, but he's not the one I've been working with most of the past several months. The same day I talked to him, I booked the packers and movers, and so I have a definite move date.

And suddenly this all became very, very real, and I realized that after I've signed the papers on Friday, I will have no more control over what happens with this house. And I have a specific day to move. And my agent won't be around. In the moment I realized all this, the ground dropped out from under me. Logically I knew that this was not true, that I still was standing in my office looking out the window, but viscerally I felt as if there was nothing solid under me. And I was terrified.

When I later described all this to a friend, she asked me how I'd dealt with that feeling. I thought about that for some time, and I realized that I dealt with it the same way that for many years I've dealt with very scary things. I observed it. I went into it. I stayed right there with it, right in the middle of it. And from there, I tried to pay attention to what I could learn from it. Where exactly in my body was I feeling this "no ground" sensation? How specifically did it feel? As I observed it and it began to change, I watched to see what changed and how it changed. And when it was over, I tried to understand what had led up to the sensation.

I think all of the things I mentioned above contributed to this feeling, together with how quickly one after the other they had happened. And I think when I really pay attention, the one "event" that most contributed to it was the realization of losing all control over my house from Friday going forward.

We have spent many years taking care of things, taking care of everything, really. We make all the major and minor decisions that go along with living a life. I realized that from the time I graduated from college, I had made all the decisions about my life: if I would go on for more education and if so, where, and if so how was I going to pay for it and for my daily expenses? I decided what my profession would be, where I would work, where I would live, how I would get myself to wherever that was. I decided when to leave a job and whether or not to look for the same kind of work. I decided on major medical treatment; whether or not to have surgery, chemotherapy, radiation, and which doctors to work with. And on and on. And suddenly during this downsizing and moving process, I was to have no control over what now happened to my house.

I'm making this sound dramatic because that's the way it has been feeling to me. And what occurs to me very strongly is that those people who work with us during this process need to be very aware of how we might be feeling. This includes downsizers, real estate agents, packers, movers, contacts at the place we're moving, and probably more. I realized that even though I knew I actually was a bit weary of taking total responsibility for myself for the last many years, the moment anyone tried, probably in many cases unconsciously, to take that responsibility away from me, I rebelled and got, in some cases, very defiant.

The feelings I'm describing may not be at all familiar to you. If that's the case, that's fine; we're all different. But in case any of this strikes a familiar chord for you, then number one, you're not the only person who has felt this way, and number two, this is important stuff to learn or relearn about yourself and cut others some slack when you want to say something you may regret later.

And for all those supporting us in making these big changes, some of us may be happy to hand over all decision making with a big sigh of relief. But it's probably a good idea to be alert for signs of how the person you're working with may be feeling, and either back off or actively include them if they seem defensive. If you do this, everything will go much more smoothly for everybody.

1. As you've been going through this downsizing process, or preparing to, are there any things you might label as "negative" that have surprised you about yourself?

2. If so, can you just forgive yourself, possibly ask others to forgive you, and then move on?

What Happens
When It's Over?

"If you knew that you are smart, creative, capable
and strong,
when would you trust yourself to begin?"

YOU AND I HAVE BEEN through a pretty long journey together. This journey began several months ago and now is nearing the end. I'm writing this on a Monday. On Friday, four days from now, escrow is supposed to close, which means at that point the buyers will own my house, and I'll be their tenant. How weird is that?

So, how am I feeling today as I begin the final week of owning the house I have dreamed of owning my entire life? Well, what I feel is... close to nothing. Nothing at all. The ideas is, "Let's just get on with it." And that keeps me most comfortable. Even though I know this will not serve me well in the long run because at some point those feelings are likely to sneak out when I least expect them. And often times this "sneaky leak" will come in the form of an overreaction to what someone has said or done, totally surprising both of us.

So, deep down, how am I feeling today? Well, the best word I can find is "panic" because it's almost too late to change my mind. I mean it would be a real mess if I changed my mind this week and decided I don't want to sell. I could say, "I think I'll just stay here, so tear up the purchase agreement, etc., etc." It would be a royal mess... AND it would be possible. But at midnight on Friday morning, it no longer will be possible. I'd have to buy the house back, and, most practically, I couldn't afford to do that. So, there it is. That's how I'm feeling. I feel as if I'm madly flailing around trying to find something to grab hold of. And there doesn't seem to be anything there.

It reminds me of the time I was preparing to go to the hospital for a pretty serious operation. I remember waking up really early the morning I was due to go in and thinking, "Well, what if I just don't go?" It's so sobering to get hold of the idea that there's something you really, really do not want to do. And you know you're going to put one foot in front of the other to take yourself there for whatever it is you really do not want to do. When and how do we learn to do this on our own? All by ourselves with no parent or guardian corralling us and carrying us to that thing that we do not want to do. It occurs to me that there must be a slight hint of masochism in our ability to do that, or a really highly developed frontal lobe that can override all the visceral sensations.

I just realized one of the things I do to get through this kind of time: I plan for what happens when it's over. In this case, on Friday evening my friends Lynn and Steve and I are going to my new home and celebrate with champagne on the balcony. So, I'm spending lots of mental time planning for that. I go back and forth trying to remember whether my champagne glasses are packed, and decide they're still in the kitchen cabinet, but I'm not sure about the little hors d'oeuvres plates in case we want snacks. And then I get to wondering how much of my life I spend planning for the thing that may happen after whatever "that thing" is that's going to happen first.

I've been wondering why I've been so tired lately. Thinking back over all the conversations we've had since the beginning of chapter one in this book, I guess it's not surprising at all. So, learn this from me: there will be some periods of time in the middle of your downsizing and preparing to move that, no matter how much sleep you get, you may be very, very tired much of the time.

All this just makes me want to go and eat a pint of ice cream.

I Don't Want To! Or Do I?

*"If you knew that you have enough time to live a
life that is even more fulfilling for you,
what would be your first step?"*

TODAY IS FRIDAY. The end of the week. In the last chapter I talked about dreading the end of the week. Now it's here. Earlier today my friends who are going with me to the new balcony to celebrate said they would do whatever would make me happy for dinner after the champagne. What immediately went through my mind was that what would make me happy is to take my house off the market and continue to live there. And that is not going to happen. So now what?

As I said, I am fascinated with those times when every cell in our body does not want to do something, and yet we inexorably keep walking toward it, step by step, arrangement after arrangement, phone call after phone call. We just keep going when somewhere inside we are screaming "I don't want to do this!" How do we learn to do this? It can't be natural.

Along these same lines I'm finding it fascinating today that I'm really tense about the possibility that escrow won't close today. Something at the last minute will bring the whole thing to a screeching halt, and I'll be back at square one trying to sell my house. So it scares me to death that that thing that I do not want to happen might not happen. I hope at least some of you can identify with this, otherwise I am going to feel just plain crazy!

I come to the conclusion that SOMETHING in us actually wants to do this thing, or, perhaps, wants to avoid the pain and fear of not doing it. And I think it might be helpful to really think about what that might be.

I am incredibly relieved that I will not have to pay the greatly increased monthly mortgage payment that will come into effect later this year. I also am relieved that I no longer will have to figure out whom to call when something starts leaking or stops working. And then I won't have to wait for them to get there to fix whatever it is, and wait and wait and wait. I no longer will have to worry about what to do about the black soot on the lime tree or whether I should just have it removed. And if I should have it removed, whom should I call to do that? And if I'm going to do that, should I just call the tree company and have them do some other major trimming while they're there? And if I did, how much would all that cost?

I'm going into lots more detail here than I suspect you're interested in, but I think it's important to do that so I can get the gut sense for how that all really feels and how relieved I am, actually, that I won't have to be concerned with it any longer.

So, if you're not looking forward to your next steps, are there any things at all that are positive about not staying where you are? You may have to really dig for this, but it will be worth it.

And here I'm feeling a need for a disclaimer. I realize that for many of you, downsizing may be a royal pain, but having gotten through it, you're actually looking forward to moving into wherever it is you're going. If so, I'm very happy for you! And even if this is the case, you're still on the precipice of a major life change, and for most of us there is at least some fear, reluctance, or trepidation associated with big changes like that. As you've probably realized from everything we've talked about so far, I'm all in favor of knowing how I'm really feeling and then working with that. I have found over and over in my life that if I will do that, I am less likely to get bushwhacked later by reactions to people or to situations that seem all out of proportion to what just happened.

So, even if you're excited to go where you're going, how are you feeling about leaving where you've been? Spend some time with this and make sure you can get as clear as possible about it. And when you are, then think about all the positive things about not staying where you are. And spend some time with that, too. And now you're as close to what's real for you as you can get, and are far more prepared for your next steps.

Be Careful What You Ask For

*"If you knew that by deliberately thinking about
something consistently
it's more likely to come about, what would you begin
to think about?"*

IN THE LAST CHAPTER we talked about how what I really wanted was to take the house off the market and continue to live there, AND how afraid I was that escrow wouldn't close even though I didn't want it to. Crazy-making, isn't it? This is not an exact quote, but I've always liked the way I remember it better, and maybe Ralph Waldo Emerson won't mind: Consistency is the hobgoblin of small minds. Isn't that great! And doesn't it just describe perfectly the way we actually live our lives from day to day?

Anyway, being completely inconsistent, I did and didn't want escrow to close last Friday. So, it didn't! The courier took the final package to the wrong place, and it ended up in Northern California rather than in Southern California. Isn't that just too perfect!! Everything got straightened out by Monday, and we did have our champagne celebration on the balcony Friday evening, but technically I still owned the house. Happy day, and oh yikes!

This kind of ambivalence is exactly what I think you should be ready for and know you're not crazy. We all go through this. I want to sell the house; I don't want to sell the house. I want to get rid of all this extra stuff and live with just enough; I want to keep most of these things that have meant so much to me. I'm looking forward to the freedom I think will come with my new living arrangement; I want to stay right here and keep things exactly the way they've been. And as Ralph Waldo Emerson realized, this is not a sign of craziness. It is a sign of being a fully alive and alert human being, active in the world of constant contradiction.

And so today I'm aware of being absolutely ready to move right now, and of wanting to lock all the doors and windows so the new owners, the packers, and the movers can't get in. Ever.

The new owners. Yes. Now they own the house, and I'm their renter. Oh yuck! Except I got a notice in the mail last night from my insurance company recommending I get earthquake insurance. And a big smile came over my face. This notice does not apply to me. Smile. Nevertheless, there are new owners. And they came by yesterday afternoon before I got home. They want to come again today and bring a designer and a contractor because, I assume, they don't actually like parts of the house too much and want to change it. This house! My house! Which is absolutely perfect, except for one or two small things here and there. And those things don't apply to me anymore. Smile.

I hope from all this you can get a clear sense of the total turmoil one can feel during this time. You're not exactly in the old place, and you're not at all in the new place. You don't want to go, and you're ready to get on with the move immediately if it were possible. You're sad and you're excited. And right now I am really, really flaky, so if that happens to you, be very careful while you're walking, driving, and taking care of important things because it can be so hard to focus when you're feeling this discombobulated.[2] I would say get as much good sleep as you can during this part of the journey.

And I think these flaky feelings are a sign of the mental and emotional turmoil I'm feeling even when I'm not aware of it. When our world is turned upside down and we're becoming unmoored from everything we've known, we're bound to feel at least a bit adrift. For those of you who like to learn something from any experience no matter how difficult, you might try doing that with all these feelings.

When I did that just now I had a vivid memory of a time when I was living in the UK. I hadn't been there very long, and I was feeling very alone and separate from everything familiar to me. I was walking down a sidewalk ("pavement" in the UK) in Bath, and happened to look down. And there, slowly crossing the sidewalk, was a perfect snail. I mean it was a cartoon image of a snail complete with a big, upright, circular shell and antennae, or whatever you call those on a snail. And I thought, "Wow! That snail takes his home with him wherever he goes!"

---

[2] Among many, many other examples, during this time I was very late for an important meeting. I am always on time or early. And one day while pulling into a parking space at my office complex, I sideswiped a car because I simply wasn't paying attention to what I was doing!

And then I realized that, actually, I do, too, in an important way. I am me no matter where I am. I take who I am, how I react to things, how I think, all my memories, everything tangible and intangible that actually makes me me. I am always "at home" just like that snail. And so are you. And so are we all, if we will just notice.

Back To Before

*If you knew that our lives only move forward, they
never go backward or remain in place,
how would you prepare for your next step into the
rest of your life?*

NINE DAYS UNTIL I MOVE. Eight days until the packers
come. My neighborhood "going away party" was last night.
Although it was hard to get through, it was a lovely thing for
my neighbors to do for me. Moving away from this neighborhood is a very hard part of my move.

About the only thing left to do is find someone to take my
rugs away. The new owners don't want them. I've asked everyone I know if they know anyone who would like the rugs. I
put one online for sale and the others for free. It's really sobering when you can't give away things you've been using
every single day! I guess I'll call "you've got junk!" or some
service and haul them away. Seems such a waste.

In fact a whole lot of what I've been going through for the
last five months seems like "such a waste." I've worried and
worried and worried. And we all know what a waste of time
and energy *that* is. I've sold for a fraction of the value and
given away thousands of dollars' worth of things that I have

acquired, in some cases, over decades. And I'm convinced that many of those things will go into someone else's basement and stay there until those people have to go through a massive downsizing. I've pretty much ignored my business because of lack of time and energy to focus on it. And now I don't even want to peek at the balance sheet for the first half of the year. In all honesty, at the moment the only good thing I can find about all this is that it's almost over, and I never have to do it again.

And I'm grateful that I'm not any older than I am going through this. It has been so hard, and I think it just gets harder and harder the older we get. So, what's my advice in addition to stop acquiring and start getting rid of stuff night now? My advice is that if you're thinking about downsizing and moving into a smaller place, begin right now. Don't wait. This is almost always true, no matter what age you are, because I think a simplified life can be a calmer and more balanced life. And I'm sure it's true if you're older and the anticipated downsizing is something that is becoming necessary. As time passes the attachment to our "things" grows, as does our attachment to the place we're living. So, the getting rid of and leaving become more and more painful. And as we get older we tend not to have the same amount of energy we had when we were younger. I have a radio show called *Prime Spark* designed for women over the age of 55. When I ask my guests if they are aware of getting older, almost to a woman they've responded that **physically** they are very aware, but not in most other ways.

And this is true for me, too. One of the things I've become very aware of is that through this process, I'm consistently tired. The other thing I've noticed is that emotions seem to cycle back; it's like I'm in a spiral of emotion, even though in many ways the whole process has seemed linear. When I woke up this morning, I realized I was deeply wishing I could go back to "before:"[3] Before I started downsizing, before I put my house on the market, before I signed the papers to move to the next place I'm going to live. I was wishing the neighborhood party last night was just another one of our parties, and we hadn't been talking about the "new owners" and when they would be moving in. Back before I felt so tired and empty much of the time, before I was worrying about how my cat is going to deal with the upcoming ordeal, before, before, before.

As is always the case when one is doing this kind of wishful thinking, at some point the cold realization hits... it will never be "before" again. It will be something else. And that probably will be OK, but it will never again be the same as "before." If any of this is true for you or if at some point it becomes true, please remember you are not alone in these feelings. I, too, have felt them. Strongly. I am feeling them as I write these words. And I think they are natural, and they remind us that we are alive and have loved aspects of our lives. And who would want it any other way? So, it means it's more painful to let go and go on to the next chapter. OK. But it's still better than hating every moment of where we are and feeling huge relief that it's almost over. And believing that deeply doesn't make the current pain any less.

That's how I see it. How do you see it?

---

[3] You may remember that in Chapter 13 we talked about how, several years ago, I had been desperately wishing I could go back to "before" the cancer diagnosis and treatment. Back to when it all seemed smooth sailing ahead with lots more birthdays and summers and Christmases to come.

Will It Be Enough?

*If you knew that your sense of feeling completely
fulfilled is just waiting inside you to be discovered,
what would your next step be?*

Saturday, July 16, 2017

THE DAY AND THE DATE MEAN that the packers come
tomorrow, and the movers come the day after that. Sigh. If by
any chance you've been doing this along with me, doesn't it
seem as if we've been doing it a LONG TIME? I actually started my first steps toward downsizing six months ago. SIX
MONTHS! That's half a year that my primary focus has been
on THIS! And today what I'm most conscious of is how scat-
tered my brain feels. Earlier this morning I took something
out of a drawer to put in the box of "I've got to remember
where this stuff is" stuff. And then I turned around and did
one other very simple thing, and then I couldn't find the
thing I'd taken out of the drawer. I looked everywhere. I
went back through all the files I'd been working with; I went
from room to room, thinking maybe I'd taken it somewhere
else. I was just ready to call a neighbor to come over and help
me look when I realized I was carrying it around with me in

my other hand. That's when I decided I needed to just sit down and write for a while.

Yesterday, generous Roy, my computer guy, came and unhooked and wrapped all the lines to the computer so the packers can pack it more easily. My friends Carol and Al came and collected my cat and took him to a kitty spa for several days so he doesn't have to endure the upcoming chaos. My friend Steve came and took some things off the walls, spackled, and painted. Remember when we talked about how much harder this all would be without the help of some close friends? Well, this week I had that in spades. In addition to all the help yesterday, earlier in the week my friend Lynn, who has several coolers, went to my house, packed all the frozen food, and took it to my new place where we put it in the much smaller freezer.

And that is what many of us will experience over and over if we are downsizing in order to move into a smaller place. Every space is going to be smaller: the kitchen, the clothes closets, the linen closets, the available wall space, and just forget about the storage space. There's likely to be nothing like that two-car garage you may be leaving. And whatever you ultimately can fit into the new place will be <u>enough</u>. I'm sure that's true, and I keep telling myself that.

As I write those last several sentences, I realize that I'm probably not done downsizing. Oh glory be. But it's probably true. I think it's a given that even though I have gotten rid of a massive amount of stuff, more will have to go once I get to my much smaller new place. I think I'm beginning to really understand when people have said that we spend the last one third of our lives getting rid of stuff. Maybe we're never really done until we "get rid of" the bodies that have been carrying us around in the world. And I, for one, am not ready to do that yet, so I guess I will just keep getting rid of things!

Very melodramatically, last evening at some point I got into a real self-pity mood, and went into thinking, "So much has been taken away from me and now my cat is gone, too." As a piece of advice, when these times come, and they probably will, feel the feelings deeply, breathe, and then get on with whatever needs to be done next. I think we don't do well if we deny these deep feelings of loss, and I don't think we do well if we wallow in them too long. And so, taking my own advice, I'm now going to stop writing and get stuff together to take to my new place before the packers arrive in the morning. And then I'm going to go home—my real home—and put more stuff in the "I've got to remember where this stuff is" box. And then I think I'll have a stiff drink, which I usually don't recommend, but every once in a great while, it might just be what's needed most.

1. What do you do when you're feeling most sorry for yourself?

2. Knowing this is not really helpful for very long, what do you do to get out of it?

Happy Is a Big Word

If you knew that your birth into this precious hu-
man life is a miracle,
what would you be most grateful for today?

"What a difference a week makes..." ♫

THE PACKERS CAME. The movers came. And in two very short days, it was all over. Well, THAT part is over. I now am living in an apartment that I can navigate by creeping along paths between boxes. I am, however, incredibly more calm and centered than I have been, maybe for months. So, for those of you who are anticipating traveling this same road that I have been describing for you, there does come an end. Not to the unpacking and arranging (I mean I assume there is an end, but I certainly can't foresee it at the moment), but to the uncertainly and upheaval of the downsizing and moving.

I will continue to proclaim my new mantra over and over: start or keep getting rid of stuff, and don't bring any new stuff in without getting rid of something that's there now. I got rid of at least 75% of what I owned. And now I have a big box on the floor in my new apartment labeled "more stuff to donate," and every day this week it has gotten fuller and fuller. I'm sure I'm going to need several more big boxes before I'm done (hint: don't break down all the boxes as you unpack).

So, I'm much calmer and more centered. Am I happy? Well, "happy" is a big word. I have my cat with me again, and he seems to be fine. In fact, he's more affectionate than he's ever been, and he's always been pretty affectionate. I uncovered the radio, so I have my wonderful classical music station again. My newspaper subscriptions have found me already, so every morning I have my newspapers. I found a lamp, so I can read in the evening with my cat by my side. And I now have the TV hooked up, so I can watch San Francisco Giants baseball and the Tour de France. All the essentials of life, really. I don't have my beautiful yard, garden and patio, but I sat on my teeny, tiny balcony last night and ate dinner. I don't have my wonderful neighbor friends, but I saw two people here this morning who remembered my name, and I remembered theirs. Basically, I'm still me, and Bu (my cat) is still Bu, and we're both healthy, sleeping and eating well, and we wake up in the morning looking forward to a brand-new day that, we're both certain, holds wondrous surprises, joys, and probably a few sorrows.

Do I feel "at home?" No, not yet. But when I say that, I remember that story I told you in Chapter 21 about the snail who takes his home with him wherever he goes. And so is it for me. The essence of me, "Sara," goes with me wherever I go. I mean there are some places I have all "my stuff" around me, and there are places I have a small suitcase of my stuff. But I'm always me. There are some places that are so familiar that they feel like part of me, but they're not really, they're just buildings and yards and patios that have become very, very familiar. And exactly the same is true for you, too.

When I went back to my "real home" this past week to leave the extra keys and garage door openers, the new owners already were there moving things in. And this reminded me of the time, many years ago, I left an organization where I had worked for a very long time. It wasn't that I was a "big cheese" there, but I had carved out a bit of a niche. And when I left at the end of the last day, I had a very clear image of a boat moving through the water, and how quickly its wake closes behind it. And I realized that that was true even for the very biggest luxury cruise ships! Even their wake closes very quickly behind them. So, no matter how long we've been someplace or what kind of impact we've made, our "wake" will close fairly quickly, and those left behind will get on with whatever happens in that place next. That may feel sad, and it's just the way it is. What that realization underscores for me is how important how we live each day is. And that is just as true in our new place as it was in our old one.

1. When you say, "This is me," what exactly do you mean? Your body? We know our bodies change every single day. Your home? Really? The essence of who you are is a combination of your living room, bedroom, furniture, yard, garden, roof, floor, lamps?

2. Take a little time and define what YOU mean by saying, "This is me."

3. Will you take that to your new place?

Moving On... Sort Of

I'VE LIVED IN MY NEW PLACE for 10 days. Is it feeling familiar yet? Well, I guess I can say it's feeling more familiar. Taking a different route home from my office every evening still feels weird. I have trouble finding stuff, but I think that's because lots of boxes still are piled in the living room and the office. But I understand better how things work and where to go to find things I need. It has not been a totally easy ride, however.

One evening this past week I had a really strong, deep feeling of wanting to "go home." I felt as if I were on a business trip, most of the work was done, and I really was ready to leave this hotel and go home. Bu, my cat, seemed to understand and feel the same way. So, I had a conversation with him, which really was addressed to myself, about how we are home. This now is home. And we can't "go home" because other people are living there. We don't even have a key for the front door. This is it. And my insides felt very empty, with a bit of a desperate clinging feeling, as if I were grasping at the sides of a very deep hole I was quickly sliding into. And so I just stayed with that for a while, and, like all good and bad feelings, they passed, and were replaced with a "this is just the way it is, Sara" feeling. Realistically, there just is no way one can live in a place for a long time and POOF! 10 days later feel "at home" in a new place. So, if you find yourself going through this kind of feeling, be gentle with yourself. I think it's natural and totally understandable. And I also think that if, when we have feelings like that, we stay with them rather than try to push them away or cover them up, they will change and we can move on in a healthy way to whatever comes next.

And what does come next? I don't know yet. I'll have to let you know.

Ignite the Light

If you knew that there isn't a specific step-by-step
plan for your life,
you get to choose it, and it's never too late,
what would you begin choosing?

I THINK THIS IS MY LAST CHAPTER. I think my "downsizing" project is complete, and now I'm into the "getting used to living here" period.

So, how is it really after one more week in my new place? Well, in all honesty, it's better. Even though it's tiny as compared with the house I left, I really do like my apartment. And I find I have everything I need. At the moment some of that "needed stuff" still is in boxes, I think, unless I sold it. Last weekend I opened and emptied all non-book boxes. This meant I had piles and piles of stuff everywhere, but it was much easier to put it away when I could organize it into "like piles," and then put it away. And I'm hoping that some of the boxes marked "books," actually contain lots of other things, too, like the unused airline ticket that I need to use to book travel sometime in the next month, I think, or I'll lose it. This coming weekend my dear friends Lynn and Steve are coming over, and we'll open the remaining boxes, even if all that stuff doesn't get put away right now.

Bu, my cat, seems calm, and has found his favorite window to "live in." In our old house he was glued to the front window from which he could see people coming and going, squirrels running around, and, when he got really lucky, the passing cat that he got to yowl at. This also is the window that he pushed the screen out of one evening, and then spent the whole night outside (he'd never been outside so far as I know) while I spent the night prowling around with a flashlight calling softly to him. I'm convinced he was hiding under a bush watching me. Best entertainment he'd had in months, I reckon.

I don't know this for sure, of course, but I suspect you can hear the lightness in my tone now, which is a sure sign that I'm feeling much better. All of that angst and pain and turmoil and endless planning is behind me. What's next? Who knows, but we never really know, do we? What I want to make sure you understand is that if you need to go through a major downsizing and move, it's better to begin earlier than later. Please read that sentence again if you know you need to do this and keep putting it off until... Thanksgiving? Christmas? Hanukkah? The birth of your third grandchild? There always will be something, and that means that when you finally get around to beginning the downsizing process, it will be that much harder than it would have been. And believe me, you don't want it to be any harder than it already is.

When I say that, I think a very understandable question would be, "how is it 'harder?'" I think that the part that's particularly harder is the emotional part. The longer we hold on to things, the harder they are to let go of. For some of us, our memories become more and more important; they more and more define who we are to ourselves. And so letting go of things that remind us of important or fun or memorable things in the past, particularly things involving cherished friends and family and deeply meaningful work, becomes harder and more painful. In addition to the emotional part, a significant downsizing and move takes a lot of energy. I don't know about you, but I've found that as I've gotten older, I just don't have the same amount of energy as I used to have. I still can do lots of the things I've always done, just not for quite as long or with as much vigor. As I talked about over the months we've been together, there were many, many times I was totally exhausted. And comparatively, I'm pretty young to have made the move I just made. So, get going!

In closing, my dear reader, I have enjoyed our time together. Some of the hours and days were very difficult for me, as you will have heard in my voice and in my stories, but knowing I could write all about it to you made the hard times a bit easier. So, thank you very, very much for listening to me. I hope you feel I also was listening to you. If there is any way I can make your own downsizing and moving process any easier, please let me know—that is the main reason I wrote this book. I deeply wanted to help anyone else preparing to go through the painful process I was going through. There are ways you can contact me listed in the last few pages of this book, and I would love to hear from you. In the meantime, take good care of yourself, and at a minimum, start or continue getting rid of as much stuff as you can right now!

*"Deep in your being there is a spark that, when dis-
covered and tended,
can ignite the light to guide you on your path to the
deep, inner sense of knowing
"I am enough."*

Three Months Later...

Before this book went to print, I wanted to talk to you one final time. I've now lived in my new place for three months. I can say with all honesty that I love my new apartment. I have about a quarter the amount of space I used to have, and I have completely enough. In fact, I love having less space. I have room for everything I need, and I know I'm no longer taking up way more than my fair share of space. Do I feel "at home" yet? Well, no, not really, but I do feel a bit more at home than I did even a couple of weeks ago. So, just hang in there! I know it probably doesn't feel like it right now, but you are going to be just fine in the not too distant future. OH, and see, I just did it! I just did one of those things I said earlier in the book is NOT HELPFUL when you're not feeling as if everything is going to be "just fine." Sorry. Just remember I'm with you all the way!

Addendum:
Supporting a
Downsizer

IT'S IMPOSSIBLE to offer suggestions that will apply to every downsizing situation. Your relationship to the person downsizing, their temperament, your temperament, the state of their health, where they're going, all these and many more variables will impact how you can successfully support the person preparing to go through a significant downsizing. Nevertheless, let's see if we can find any suggestions that might apply to many different situations.

One of the people I spoke with in preparing to write this book was Maria Quinby, owner of On the Move. Maria helps people plan for a downsizing and move, and can be actively involved all along the way. She helped me downsize; I could not have done it without her. She is a true professional. Maria said that, not surprisingly, many people want to "age in place," and not move from the home where they may have been for many years. Sometimes that is possible, and sometimes it is not. By the time it may not be possible, a significant downsizing and move can be extremely painful and overwhelming. In situations like this, perhaps the most support others can offer is to listen to the stories and feelings of the person needing to move while taking care of all that needs to be taken care of. Even in these situations, however, it will be easier on the person if their desires and preferences are taken into account to the extent possible. Sentences like "Mother, you don't need that old thing," can be very hurtful and only add to the pain the person already is feeling.

Perhaps a more common situation than this downsizing of necessity, is that of us aging Baby Boomers deciding we are ready to downsize and move into a smaller place. While it may be emotionally easier to downsize when one is choosing to do so, it does not necessarily mean that it will be any less painful. The person downsizing still will come face to face with years and years of memories they will have to get rid of.

There may be toys and other things that were important to their children while they were growing up. There may be wedding presents they were given, and the giver was very important to them at some point. There may be items acquired all over the world from never-to-be forgotten trips or visits. For most people there are family pictures of major and minor events that still are fondly remembered. For many there will be things that belonged to their parents who are still living or, more often, have died some time ago. And on and on.

For most of us, at least some of these kinds of things can be very painful and sad to have to part with even if we've made the choice to downsize and move. In fact, lots and lots may need to go. And here is the first "don't do:" unless it is a rare, one-of-a-kind, very valuable item, never try to talk the downsizer into keeping something they have decided to part with. That decision may have been very difficult. Don't make them make it twice. An alternative is to offer to take the item and sell it, and give them the proceeds rather than watch it end up in the trash pile or in the garage sale where it is likely to bring about $1.95.

As I talked with people who had downsized or were planning to do so in the near future, they had assumed, perhaps for many years, that they were saving things for their children, only to find that their children wanted nothing. And this sometimes was true even if the adult children didn't want their parents to get rid of some of the things!

So, if you are an adult child of a parent whom you are helping downsize, you don't need to feel guilty about not wanting to take things, even if they are things that were very important to you at some point in your life or are very important to your parents. On the other hand, don't make them feel guilty for getting rid of your "treasures" that they simply will not have room for. Just as they are doing, you need to let things go by selling them, donating them, or putting them out for the trash.

For adult children or other family members or friends who are helping with the downsizing, this is not the time to identify things that you would like, either now or in the future. If the downsizers ASK if there are any things you'd like to have now or later, say what those things are and why you would like to have them. Keep it to a few items and express thanks for the givers' generosity. And here is a perfect example of how each situation is different: When I was going through my downsizing, I loved it when friends mentioned something they would like because I had to get rid of so much, and I found it far less painful when someone I know and care about took the item. So, as the supporter of the downsizer, you need to be the sensitive one. They very possibly are in emotional overwhelm and may not have the same level of sensitivity to others that they usually do. You need to be the one to "read" the situation carefully and act in a sensitive, helpful way. And if you feel that for whatever reason you can't do that, then try to find someone else to help the downsizer because you may just be making the process more difficult for the person.

Earlier in the book I suggested to the downsizer to make a list of the specific things they'd like help with. If they haven't done that, you might ask them if they'd be willing to do that so you know what they really would like you to do. It's not helpful to either one of you to say that you'd be happy to help any time; they should just let you know. In that moment they may not be able to think of one or two things, and they may be reluctant to pick up the phone and call later to ask for help. For many of us, that is a very difficult thing to do. Plus, we can't be sure someone means it since it is so common to hear people say, "Let me know how I can help."

It's best to let the downsizer take the lead on how they feel about moving out of where they are and into where they're going. If they're happy and/or relieved, then keep encouraging and saying things like, "Oh it's going to be so much easier to take care of the smaller place!" Or, "It's so great that you won't have to worry about this big yard any longer." Listen to them and encourage those things that they have identified as being positive or a relief.

If, however, they are really sad about leaving where they are and/or are not happy about what they're moving into, then DO NOT say things like, "Oh it's going to be such a relief to get out of here!" Or, "You'll see; you're going to love it there!" Those kinds of sentences are not helpful, can be hurtful, and can really annoy the person. Don't make this difficult situation worse for them.

Always ask first, but often one of the most helpful things you can do is take things away that need to go away. For example, if there are several piles that need to go to Goodwill, offer to drop them off and give the downsizer the tax receipt. If there are boxes and boxes of books that need to find a new home, offer to take them to the local library or find a place in your area that accepts used books. If you have the time and are willing, offer to help with a garage sale if the person is going to have one. Most of us cannot manage a large garage sale on our own physically, let alone emotionally. And if you can't help before or on the day, offer to bring food and/or drinks to the "workers" if that's doable. This is important: Always find out where the downsizer would like you to take things that are being donated. Unless the person doesn't care, don't assume it will be fine to take the things to your favorite charity shop or nonprofit. It may be important to the person giving away all those things that the things go to a particular organization. Many of us find it much easier to get rid of things we need to get rid of and/or aren't using when we know where they're going and we support that cause.

Professional Downsizers

For professional Downsizers whose job it is to help people downsize and move, you have an incredibly difficult role to play well. On the one hand, you often may need to be ruthless in helping the person who has hired you get rid of a massive amount of possessions, depending on how much they have and the size of the place they're moving into. And that's what they've hired you to help them do. For you this may be a "project" among many others you're managing at the same time. But for each person you're helping, this is their life, and the depth of your empathy may make the difference in how painful the process is for them. You may not have time to listen to every story about each item that the person picks up, but if you don't have time to listen to some stories, you've overbooked yourself.

It's also important for you professional Downsizers to ask and/or to stay alert for how involved the person you're working with wants to be in the downsizing process. They may want to just oversee the process at arm's length, which may make your job easier. But if they want to be very involved and make all the decisions about what stays and what goes, it's their life, and it's their stuff, and it's not your right to try to insert yourself into that process. I know of one couple who downsized from a large house to a small apartment. When they moved in, they had about three times more than would fit in the apartment. That was a real pain for them; but they wanted to be in charge, and that was their right.

In some situations it may be helpful for the person downsizing to rent an external storage space for at least a short time, and they may need help in doing this. The external space sometimes can act as a "stepping stone" to getting rid of things. If this is done, it is important to set a specific date when the contents of the space are reviewed. Usually, with the passage of some time, some of the things can be donated or thrown out. If this process is continued, at some point the space will no longer be needed.

Real Estate Agents

If the people downsizing are selling their house, their Real Estate Agent will play a very important role at some point. The agent also can have a big impact on how the person who is downsizing and selling feels during the process. It is important to let the person selling make all the decisions they want to. In so many ways the downsizer is relinquishing control over aspects of their life for which they may have been responsible for years and years. For many, this will be very difficult to deal with, and potentially quite depressing. If the person wants the agent to take over and "just do it," fine. Your job will be easier. It is important, however, to find out to what extent the downsizer wants to be involved in things like whether or not to stage the home, what alterations inside and out need to be done, how much new landscaping should be undertaken. The person also should know the cost of each of these items. Granted, these costs will be deducted from the profits and, therefore, have a direct impact on the taxes owed. Nevertheless, the current owner has a right to know how much each of the things is going to cost.

It also is important to remain as positive as possible about the house. During downsizing and preparing to sell, the downsizer may hear a constant stream of all the things that are wrong with their "stuff" and with their house. For whatever reasons, at some point the person made the decision to buy the things in the house and to decorate it. It can be very hurtful to hear a constant stream of all the things wrong with the house and its contents. I remember a couple of times when I thought, (and I don't think I said, but who knows?), "Look, this is my house and I LIKE it the way it is. If I didn't, I would have changed it!"

For all of you who are in any way supporting a downsizer, your job is very hard. There may be many times when you feel overwhelmed with impatience and frustration. The closer to the person you are, the more likely you will have some of these feelings, AND the more hurtful your insensitive, quick comment may be. If you've been hired by the person to help, this may be one of many clients you have and simply don't have time to "dawdle" with the person as they tell their stories and try to remember where something is. How you deal with the frustrations and delays, however, may make a big difference to how painful the whole experience is to the person you're helping.

Acknowledgements

The only way I got through my downsizing and move was with a lot of help from my friends (Sorry Beatles; mine was more than "a little."). Lynn and Steve were with me from the very beginning to the very end, if I'm at an end yet. Steve doesn't think so. Whenever they come over, he still brings his tools. And usually uses them. In addition to Lynn and Steve, Corinne and Martha worked hard from early morning to late afternoon helping with the garage sale. And I don't know what I would have done without Ken and Maxine, my next-door neighbors, who welcomed me into their house many times a day for a drink, a meal or a good conversation. And a big thank you to Carol and Al who came and got Mr. Bu and took him to a kitty spa during the packing and moving. I worried more about how Bu was going to get through the move than I did about me! Carol and Al made that part very easy.

My editor and now friend, Amy Collette of Positively Powered Publications, was with me every single step of the way from the very first words I put on paper to the delivery of this completed book. Never once did I feel that Amy suspected I might not get the book written or that it was unimportant. She was unfailingly positive about how helpful the book would be for people as they prepared to go through what I was going through.

My designer, Melody Christian of Finicky Designs, was 100% all in from the very beginning. Selecting one book cover from the several Melody designed for me was very difficult. And not only is she a brilliant designer, she was very patient.

I am grateful for all the people who were willing to speak to me about their own experiences with downsizing, either as someone who had just been through it or as someone who is involved professionally with people as they downsize. Many people were very generous with their time and with their own experiences. And for that I am very appreciative.

And finally, thank you to all my friends who were so supportive during many very difficult months. It is a huge testament to them that they still are my friends after my many days of anger, sadness, depression, and overall snippiness. Thank you all.

And as a postscript, thank you to Saint Joseph. If you don't understand what this means, you will as you read the book.

About the Author

Sara B. Hart, PhD, founded her management consulting company, Hartcom, 20 years ago to focus on people development, leadership development, coaching, and team building inside organizations. Much of Sara's work centers on how to build a Thinking Environment (www.timetothink.com) in which people can do their best thinking. Sara is also a speaker and a coach, and hosts a radio show called Prime Spark, designed for women over the age of 55.

A special project she has had for many years is called the Sign of Enough, which helps us answer the question "How will I know when I have enough?" Sara's interest in this idea has grown over the years as the economic inequality in the United States and around the world has become more significant, our overconsumption continues to place our environment at risk, and many of us seem to have forgotten what's really most important as we strive for more and more and more.

Sara loves to go on bike rides, walks, to attend movies, concerts, opera, theatre, and especially to have dinner with friends. She lives with her cat, Mr. Bu, in Los Altos, California.

A note from Sara:

I would love to hear about your experiences with downsizing. If you'd like, please send me an email at sarahart@hartcom.com. And if there's any way I can help you as you prepare to downsize or to go through the process, please let me know. I'm here.

If you want to continue this journey with me, be sure to keep your eye out for the next installment in a book that, for the moment, I'm calling *The Renegade Rabbit*. (If you want to know why, you'll have to read the book.)

Made in the USA
Middletown, DE
29 November 2021

53337477R00076